LEY LINES AND THE RUSTLING OF CEDAR

By the same author:

Transit

LEY LINES AND THE RUSTLING OF CEDAR

NILOOFAR FANAIYAN

Ley Lines and the Rustling of Cedar
Recent Work Press
Canberra, Australia

Copyright © Niloofar Fanaiyan, 2018

ISBN: 9780648257950 (paperback)

 A catalogue record for this book is available from the National Library of Australia

All rights reserved. This book is copyright. Except for private study, research, criticism or reviews as permitted under the Copyright Act, no part of this book may be reproduced, stored in a retrieval system, or transmitted in any form by any means without prior written permission. Enquiries should be addressed to the publisher.

Cover Cover design: Recent Work Press
from a design created by Vilmosvarga - Freepik.com
Set by Recent Work Press
Internal photographs © Niloofar Fanaiyan, 2018

recentworkpress.com

Contents

aqueducts and ley lines	2
On the first night...	3
Rain dance—1	4
The first song...	6
And then it rains	8
the rust red bark...	9
Two rows of Norfolk Island pine...	10
a sailor with no boat...	11
A ship's horn sounded...	13
Saturn hovers near the moon...	14
Palm	15
Epidermis and rhytidome touch	17
Mirrors in the garden	18
Willow	20
Sentinel at the foot of the marble stairs,	21
Layers	23
Two small green lizards...	24
Two ancient cypresses	25
Royal Poinciana	26
orange blossoms speckle the hedgerow...	28
Frangipani 1	30
Frangipani 2	32
Vitex trifolia,	33
Oak and acorn	34
Jacaranda	35
Driving on the winding dirt...	37
Whirling dervishes	38
The Fig Tree—Prologue	40
The Fig Tree—1	41
The Fig Tree—2	42
Bird that dwells in a mysterious tree	44
Instructions for building a home—	46
in bluegrey sunset...	47
Life (for K.A.)	48

The tree line is not a line...	49
Cypress	51
Ash	52
The Moon's Weaving (For M.D.)	54
Rattling storms pierce the senses	55
Deodar	56
Afterword	58
Acknowledgements	59

aqueducts and ley lines

the arteries are under their roots, clawed into the dirt and soft grass, lifting their tresses, sage-like in the muted beams' moonglow, even as your feet tread the earth and slowly absorb magnetic forces flowing measure by measure, however microscopic those measures may be, into your body, along your skin below your skin, through your blood stream, and out through your pores your eyes your breath—it permeates the space you walk in until your being is breathing the ley, and you have become part of the line

On the first night the bird circled the waters from far above—we were becalmed—on the second night two birds sailed in wide gyrations above the river, closer now—we were floating along an estuary—on the third night two great birds flew in circles against a pale blue sky, moving closer, then far away, then close again, then far away again—we were standing in a field of green waves—when I woke up all I could see were those two black shapes, as though the image was imprinted onto my irises.

Rain dance—1

The clinging filaments of her voice
permeate all things blue
as hearts fall and other shades are lost
before the horizon—

فرش آب در دامنۀ آسمان انداختند،
تارهای آبی در ابریشم افق موج میزنند——

Farshe aab dar damaneye aseman andakhtand, tarhaye aaby dar abrishame ofogh moj meezanand—they have laid a carpet of water at the skirt of the mountain, webs of blue wave within the silk of the horizon

silken threads rise
and rise again, the earth a loom with no back
and no front, an invisible frame.
A sprig of bluebells floats in her hair,

woven in the night
the weaving was accompanied by song
and dance—at one end of the bridge

یکی بود، یکی نبود
at the other end of the bridge
یکی بود، یکی نبود——

Yeky bood, yeky nabood—there was one, and there was none (traditional Persian introduction to oral fairy-tales)

چشمهای دیروز در آبی دریا،
باران فردا در آبی هوا –

Chashmhaye deerooz dar aabiye darya, barane farda dar aabiye havaa—the eyes of yesterday are in the blue of the sea, the rain of tomorrow is in the blue of the sky

and today is lost in the air between.
The moon flutes a winding breeze,
disrupts the many shades of blue,
and the rain swings around the loom—

باران می‌رقصد و می‌پرسد:
کدام آب است و کدام هوا،
کدام زمین است و کدام فضا؟

Water and air whisper against the skin
of her hand, her feet, her face.
She hums and whirls,
sky and sea,
she is blue.

Baran meeraghsad va meeporsad: kodam aab ast va kodam havaa, kodam zameen ast va kodam fazaa—the rain dances and asks: which is water and which is air, which is earth and which is space?

The first song began with a piccolo pitched call repeating itself through the haze of hypnagogic dreaming—we were compelled to lift our heads, almost to join in with the song, to become the instruments that would change this ensemble into a full orchestra—

at exactly nine minutes and ten seconds into Mendelssohn's violin concerto in E minor, allegro molto appassionato, I woke up and the birds took off and we flew as one with the rising currents—

make sure your wing-tip is touching mine, so when the rain starts you'll know I'm here, one hooded crow said to another hooded crow—the clouds had materialized in a jagged streak above the mountains in the distance and were converging overhead—*you haven't slept in days, how will we make it through the storm?*

five minutes and thirty seconds into Bruch's violin concerto in G minor, allegro moderato, a small tornado formed in the middle of the avenue and spiraled quickly out of control—it carried all sentient beings to the Eagle nebula where butterflies were quickened and reimagined—

a new opus began to take shape around the voices that were born in the nebula, synchronised and syncopated as the score demanded—

all the while musicians flew the spiraled path,

wing-tip to wing-tip

And then it rains

The gnarled branches, extending from a great twisting body, reach out to the world in all directions, their small glossy sage-like leaves perched along—she stretches deep into the mountain and no-one knows how long she has been there, what she has seen, what she is waiting for—a mottled cat of black and white lays in her shadow, staying out of the sun and away from other cats—a gardener checks the branches for any fruit and then moves on—the haze is shifting on the horizon, the dessert dust almost tangible in the air—the birds overhead break formation and the cat runs for greater shelter—someone crushes her fallen leaves underfoot in the rush for cover—the smell of olive oil is lifted up by the dusty wind, and then it rains.

the rust red bark of the giant eucalypt seemed to reflect
a blending of the picture before it— red petals against cream-
   coloured stone—
heated by the fires of earth and sky the two seemed
as though paint had been poured into paint—the blood of sacrifice
into the hazy pages of the future, melded, even as the rooster calls—
and when the rain begins the man with an umbrella offers shelter
to the man without, together they stand between the giant and the
   sepulchre—
red petals against cream-coloured stone—there is no fragrance here,
only bowed heads

Two rows of Norfolk Island pine swayed in tandem as the westerly wind
blew in from the bay—their triangular forms almost bopping—
a couple of shamrock parrots (who also looked like they should be on an island in the Pacific)
circled one pine tree before perching on another—
when the rain stopped you could smell the bitter citrus oils from the sour orange
fallen to nestle on the soft grass, small and potent,
stark chalcedony against an emerald carpet—
the weather is being dramatic one parrot said to the other from their superior vantage point,
it is only appropriate the other responded—
a gardener moved about below, quickly and surely, in the aftermath
as the ships entered the bay

a sailor with no boat climbed to reach the other side of the mountain, avoiding cyclists and other pedestrians on the way—in order to sail again, he had been informed, he would have to first master all other forms of transport—of course, no-one yet knew that, ironically, he gets car-sick—as he neared the mountain-top a whiff of the sea floated under his nostrils and he closed his eyes in fond remembrance of his many adventures, notably sailing through a niagara—that is when he walked into the road-block, an old house of impressive proportions—the caretaker stood by the door and watched him warily, *you will need to go around*, he croaked, *didn't you see the sign?!*—the sailor pressed his palm against his sore knee where it had collided with solid brick—it seemed like it would be a while longer before he would sail again, and so he sang, *you are a shadow on the water, a feather floating past my face, a glimmer in a darkened room, the smell of rain on a dry day*

A ship's horn sounded as they all shifted slightly in the water. The light shifted again—*cheshmha rowshan* she had said—and it felt as though the lit up city was many eyes lit up with wonder. Meanwhile, the tree drooped to both sides as if it bore a heavy burden. *They've cut him* he said, and it was true—the tree bore scars—he looked heavy with years, with duty, with love, and so he drooped to both sides near the top of an ancient mountain at the edge of a wilderness. Almost, in a way, he was bowing to hide his secrets, reflecting the levitation of the white city in the distance. And as the lowered branches whispered to the hooded crows passing overhead, my spirit lifted with the fading, with the darkening of the sky, with the clearing of the air. Now it is dark all around and the city, black, is lit up like a field of fireflies. Or is it a sea on fire? It's hard to tell where the city begins and ends—lamps descend along and around, onto piers, and follow the ships into the sky. *I like city lights* he said. And now we didn't know which way was up and which way was down—the night inverted.

Saturn hovers near the moon, a mild cosmic storm ruffles its rings in rotation—or so it seems through the lens—behind my head the gnarled fingers of an olive tree rustle and reach out over the city below, fingertips translucent in the light pollution—the city is about to take off into outer space. Who knows when we might see each other again? The olive tree thought she had seen it all.

Palm

They tried to keep out the world with a wall, with concrete, grey and granulated—the wall slowly became their world, seemingly solid, decorated with cartoons and slogans of different colours—then the world began to eat the wall, porous, grown over by the gently encroaching morning glory, the cat bathed in the luxurious sun not bothering to even wink at the little birds feeding nearby—palm trees followed the shore and breathed life into clusters of homes, popping up amongst wall fragments and became garden features, always giving and needing very little in return—in the end the wall became a gate, a window, and a twist in the plot.

Epidermis and rhytidome touch, blood and sap flow somewhere underneath—these seemingly imperfect surfaces—a flimsy armour embracing wood or flesh, beings and creatures separate from the rest, while oxygen courses through veins and sap wood and the spaces between them—bowed head beneath bowed branches breathes, and smiles at the sweetness of pine—epidermis and rhytidome touch, and lean against each other—galaxies exhale under a warm afternoon sun.

Mirrors in the garden

آفتاب که میرود مهتاب میاید،
آینهٔ همان است که نور میبارد

Aftab ke miravad mahtab miayad, ayneye haman ast ke noor mibarad—as the sun departs the moon arrives, it is the mirror of the one that rains light…

violet petals hesitate then turn slowly inwards
as claws tap against ghostly pale bark
as a nightingale perches on the bough of a gum tree,
weeping tresses of a nearby willow wave in their direction,
'you're far from home' says the tree to the bird,
white light spills through black leaves,
past blinking black eyes,
onto the garden below where

با سرهای پایین گلها در خواب——

Ba sare payin golha dar khab—with heads bowed the flowers asleep—

'They fell asleep,' nightingale swoops over the flowers
and returns to alight his makeshift throne,
the willow rustles, 'the sun has left us all'
flora and fauna murmur in accord,
a dwindling piece of universe blazes across the sky—

کوکب میشود شهاب،
علامت همان است که نور میبارد——

Kokab mishavad shahab, alamate haman ast ke noor mibarad—it is the sign of the one that rains light…

and a dull claw scrapes black lines in frustration,
the gum tree disconcerted
by the cutting of its white flesh,

wings fold, manoeuvre through branches,
landing above and below, magpies warble:

بیدار شوید! بیدار شوید!

Bidar shavid! Bidar shavid!—Awake! Awake!

The roses stir, lilies roll in the pond,
and purple shadow sweetly kisses their reflection—
آینهٔ همان آینه است که نور میبارد——
and a gumnut comes loose under the weight
of a shifting owl,
and the light of the light of the light ripples
across the eye of the nightingale,

Ayneye haman ayne ast ke noor mibarad —it is the mirror of that mirror that rains light—

a drop of the wave drops past purple petals,
sinks into the yellow heart—a lily blinks—

پر پرنده و پر گیاه و برگ و چوب و نفس و هوا،
علامات همان آینه است که نور میبارد،

Pare parandeh o pare giah o barg o choob o nafas o hava, alamaate haman ayne ast ke noor mibarad—feathers of birds and petals of plants and leaves and wood and breath and air, the signs of that mirror that rains light

roses bend their thorns,
frangipani unfurl from mourning,
eagle soars and raises his voice:

ای گلستان بشر بیدار شو
که آفتاب فردا در قلب گلها است.

Ey golestane bashar bidar sho / ke aftabe farda dar ghalbe golhast—oh flower-garden of humanity awake / for the sun of tomorrow resides in the hearts of flowers.

And the light of the light of the light brightens
as the sun returns.

Willow

They saw her run but they could not stop her—when the alarm sounded, when the walls shook, when the roaring of the river reverberated through the haze of summer heat—she was with the children and then she was gone, running across the field, tearing through tall poppies, red silken petals strewn in her wake.

They saw her enter but they could not stop her—a shuddering wall of expanding river was accelerating towards them, the mountain protested, the children's eyes widened—she was struggling towards the far bank, mostly submerged, seeming to dance with the waves that lifted her arms and made her sway.

They saw her take root mid-stream and face the flood—and she grew—and she absorbed the excess water—and while the river expanded it stopped short of the village—now she embraced both land and river, now she rested in the shadow of mountains—her tears were beads of golden green threaded to her hair and floating about her as a veil.

Cool autumn air came shushing through that veil, the last of the poppies swam past on their way to the sea, and the child Gabriel sat on a boulder beating his drum, waiting for her to sing.

Sentinel at the foot of the marble stairs,

of slender and elegant frame, bowing towards the Shrine, she is always leading the way—as I approach I am compelled to pause—she stands on the path so there is no avoiding her—we have a ritual, she and I—she demonstrates reverence, silence, and reminds me of the wilderness both within and without—I acknowledge her presence, admire her beauty, and take a moment to emulate her—at times she seems dwarfed by the old giants that loom overhead, but she is protected by their looming and only the smallest birds accompany her—ultimately it is the butterflies that are her greatest and most unusual ornaments, symmettrical in wing-span and golden like the dome that she bows towards.

Layers

There is a calm directing of forces, of thoughts, of emotions, towards a single place and non-place, of leaning cypress and a dissipating early morning fog.

There is that shade of blue again, running like a vein, away and back again, carrying oxygen and nutrients to the flowers stretched out in the pattern before me.

There is a particle of fibre on the edge of a woollen tassel—it vibrates in a secret dance as though moving to every sigh, every ragged intake of breath, every undisclosed murmur.

There are layers of prayer that resonate in the walls, that cling to door handles and illuminate the borders—years upon souls, love upon doubt, questions upon certitude.

Open your eyes a mere slit, let the air brush past your irises, let your hands fall with the tide, let the light lift.

There is a calm directing of forces

Two small green lizards racing each other in and out of the hollows and nooks of the olive tree—they scuttle over a very large node then pause as they sense a pair of eyes watching them from a short distance—just as they slithered with great speed, so now they are caught in time, the curious gaze of another creature having transformed them into elegant jade ornaments, perhaps placed in this garden by an artist who was passing through—and just as I write this my hand halts, my body is paralysed—I am a statue of a woman writing her reflections, carved by an artist and placed in this sun room by another artist who was passing through. I, too, freeze under the curious gaze of another creature.

Two ancient cypresses

They are old friends—
their faces bared to each other,
their heads touching slightly,
foliage intertwined.
They loom over the stone cottage, protecting
the garden that has grown around them—
they harbour birds from near and far,
amongst the visitors
amongst the fruit trees
and roses in full-bloom in the afternoon sun—
one visitor steps over a hedge
and bends to smell the warm sweet rose—
another visitor sits by the well
and talks to an old friend about smelling roses.

Royal Poinciana

Two lizards stared up from garden ruffage at the cloud of flames growing throughout the branches overhead—*how long has he been here* one of them asked, *look at the way he displays his plumes like a peacock* the other commented, ignoring the question—he was glowing in the morning light, fernlike feathery leaves translucent curtains of rainforest green spreading through the sky in every direction creating a dappled umbrella over the garden floor—time and again he held out his flameflowers as a tribute to the glorious sunrise, and time and again he shed those ornaments as a sacrament before the ageless sea.

orange blossoms speckle the hedgerow
as they fall from the trees along the border, their perfume
summons the ladies of the crag—one white shawl is caught
on the hedge as its wearer carefully collects the blossoms
and places them into a small muslin bag—

crunching gravel warns her of others nearby
and she drops a blossom onto the gravel in alarm—
her own shadow obscures the shapes in the lamplight
as she bends to find her lost treasure—eyes closed,
the perfume of evening prayers, afternoon tea, a mid-day stroll

rises from the red stones at her feet—*orange blossoms*
a pilgrim murmurs, on their way home for the night

After the storm the pebbled path was strewn with juniper berries
fallen from the arms of these wild dancers, windswept
and struck with hailstones, but still distinctly cypress-like –

after dawn prayers someone sat in the shadows beneath these columns
sketching the small pointed leaves like rosemary and thyme
and watching the waning sun out of the corner of her eye –

after the desert three thriving junipers emerge from the rocks
to cleanse the air and bless the field, in the summer heat
as she pauses on the stone path to notice the three

Frangipani 1

This blossom that lies before me—silken cream petals that gently curve around a heart of noonday sun—fell with its brothers and sisters from these elongated branches of grey, mid-rotation at a moderate height—ornaments dotting the lawn like the stars dotting the sky, they are aligned with the arms in arabesque, indicating the way, (in case you lost sight of the red gravel, or if your compass was hindered by a glitch and ended up pointing you towards this flower), this flower that lies before me.

Frangipani 2

Two heads lean towards each other—one of golden curls and one of earthy whorls—soft whispers, bell-like voices chime and weave back and forth as curls and whorls nod and turn. A single frangipani on the desk between them—a friendship otherworldly, a bond that endures—transforms with the moments, as questions are answered, with a love that is both golden and earthy. A little blue bird taps at the window sill—the clock strikes twelve, the workshop is quiet, but the perfume of frangipani still lingers.

Vitex trifolia,

the young ones pass by as your colour changes from purple to purple, from season to season they trek beneath your foliage, sometimes laughing sometimes sombre, always contemplating in your shadow—two ladies sing and twirl while a third watches and smiles and picks up a leaf of deep Byzantium—body and branches are twisted as though being wrung to dry by the wind, and you scatter blossoms across the pebbled path for the young ones to admire

Oak and acorn

A little boy picked up an acorn and a pebble and regarded them as equal items of interest—the oak tree was not amused—he placed them both on the grass and went back for more. His parents tried to explain that the pebbles needed to stay where they were but the little boy was already on a mission—besides, after moving them to one side he could always move them back—more fun. The oak tree observed this interplay with some trepidation—if the acorns got moved too far then the crows might not find them. Just then another little boy came ambling down the path—the oak tree sighed and dropped a few more acorns.

Jacaranda

That split-second before the fall
elongates into minutes then hours as you replay it over and over—
a sudden jolt in the flow of time and the slow-motion begins—
the 'everyday' flickers—the shapes around you are a blur—
there is no sound (as though you are submerged under ten feet of
    water).

That split as the grip loosens—
there will be pain for you both—as you replay it over and over,
first comes fear then resignation—an offbeat lack of commotion—
on an ordinary day speckled with wind-traffic-coffee—
she will let go as she has done before, her purple children

born as ornaments of the sky but destined
to adorn their mother's feet

Driving on the winding dirt we pause at a bend, a Eucalyptus cluster
in the early morning mist, a pale sun through the trunks of paper white
streaked with grey calligraphy, a primal poem I cannot read but hear fragments of in the misty silence—
Hallowed earth, weave your magic,
Atoms, let down your veil.

The scent of pine trees off the beaten path approaches like footsteps
falling on a bed of pine-needles, cones elegantly formed to resemble
a sweet and tangy tropical fruit, a taste I have known but cannot remember in the cold air of January—
Hallowed earth, weave your magic,
Atoms, let down your veil.

Among rosemary webs of intricate architecture glisten with the captured
early morning dew, and children crouch in the shade watching for ideas,
the architect ambles round a sprig and begins a new structure in patterns we are still to comprehend—
Hallowed earth, weave your magic,
Atoms, let down your veil.

Eleven-o'clock-sun applies heat to lavender and aromatic oil particles
disperse to encounter man-with-camera, the insouciant humming of bees
further draws him around to capture the perfect marriage of blue and red, sacrificed for a new creation—
Hallowed earth, weave your magic,
Atoms, let down your veil.

Driving on the winding dirt we pause at another bend,
and watch the whirling dervishes frozen in time.

Whirling dervishes

At first you notice them only as a cluster scattered across the green, and yet they are
in position as they have been for aeons—
in their bearing you see humility and honour—
ancient and scarred from the battle for survival, their bodies are twisted mid-whirl,
arms extended and heads tilted to one side—
in their dance they are unconcealed and vulnerable—
they circumambulate the beloved, tresses open and flowing about the palimpsests
they have become, held in eternal homage—
in their stillness you feel the swelling of the universe—
a southerly breeze lifts the olive leaves as though the instruments have struck up
once again, wrinkled branches quaver momentarily—
and in their silence you hear the word sanctified
as the music of heaven rises from the belly of the earth.

The Fig Tree—Prologue

Filigree in the sky—that is what I saw the last time I was here, standing under the looping branches of the fig tree—the grand bowl of its body resting on ancient land.

'Will you speak to me?' I asked, feeling hopeful in the asking. But it seemed to be the wrong question. I laid my fingers against the cracked skin of its trunk and thought. Then I tried again, 'How did you get here?'

The little clusters of fruit shifted in the wind, and the shapes of the filigree were distorted momentarily. Yellow snapdragons waved nearby at the small golden cypresses that lined the paths. 'Tell me your name...'

Undulating vibrations drifted then soared through space, softly brushing the corners of the room, silencing the air itself till all was still but for the undulations—the tones, a sacred longing, expanded and filled the chamber—souls were caught in suspension, synapses hummed, and inner eyes beheld a glimmer—we were transported, a soft green canopy at the edge of awareness—the final note echoed

The Fig Tree—1

At the beginning of that which had no beginning a seed was parted from the broken flesh of its fruit—it had slowly ripened on a branch stretched out from under other branches, and eventually fallen when a bird fixated on it (this one still bore claw marks)—a gale of unusual force passed through the valley lifting all manner of stuff from the earth—this seed was also taken up and carried over the hills, along the shore, through numerous fields—at one point the seed thought it could hear heavenly melodies being played on a reed pipe far below—one day the gale came to a sudden halt and all manner of stuff fell—the seed landed in a soft bed of rich soil, but there was no music.

Sometime later as it became a sapling and as it grew and dug its roots deeper into this new land, it became aware of a family of trees nearby—they seemed to twist and whisper constantly—there were no people, and there was no music—from time to time rain would shower down, birds would visit, the seasons would change—when the sapling had become a tall fruit bearing tree, a little girl began to visit—she would lay little stones near its trunk, play till she was tired, fall asleep beneath its branches, and still there was no music.

Dust took over the skies, covered leaves and branches and the ground, and darkened the orchard for a while—a young woman watered the tree and helped it survive those days—at the dawn of another day the tree was swayed by a tired breeze and on that breeze it sensed the drawing near of people—they who had greatly suffered, they who could barely stand—and as they drew near the tree braced its roots deep in the ground and braced its trunk, sturdy, in the air—

He who had suffered most sat and leaned against that warm brown trunk, and one youth sat in its shade, and another stood guard nearby—

Someone began to play the reed pipe again.

The Fig Tree—2

The orchard at the edge of a remote mountain range had five guardians—they each tended the different plants: delicate flowers, plants for extreme climates, robust but temperate trees and bushes, the creepers and climbers (both decorative and otherwise), and the fruit trees.

Every day, at the hour after morning rain, a heavenly music could be heard, floating and swelling from over the mountain, the sound of a reed pipe that at times could have been a human voice.

On a strange and cloudy day, when no music was heard, the youngest guardian, a girl named Hafiz, was entrusted to carry a fig sapling to a new orchard—carrying the sapling in a special sling filled with rich soil, she bade farewell to the other guardians—she travelled for many days and nights till she lost count of how many days and nights she had been travelling, and when she could not find shelter she would keep herself awake by humming the music of the reed pipe to the starry sky.

The sapling remained small (it would flourish once replanted)—Hafiz, on the other hand, was aging rapidly away from her home—she would stop at every village, barter her skills with plants and botany for food and shelter, and ask about the new orchard.

One night, resting by a river, she was overtaken by the whisperings of old trees—as old as herself—but this chatter was not born on the air, it was hushed by the soil beneath her feet—she gathered herself and followed the ley line till she came upon a gathering of olive trees, and just beyond this conclave was the promising ground she had been looking for—Hafiz delivered the sapling to the earth, just above an aqueduct and near the chatty ley line, and with a word of thanks to the olives, retreated to finally rest by the sea.

Ages past and Hafiz's trust became a grand tree—troubles rolled by and overhead but the angry voices and noises were distant—even the silence seemed muffled—through the surreal haze a young boy would ride his horse through the field and parallel to the aqueduct, would pause during droughts to water the tree, would check the branches when winds grew wild—at the dawn of another day the tree sensed the drawing near of people who had greatly suffered, they who could barely stand—

He who had suffered most sat and leaned against that warm brown trunk, and one youth sat in its shade, and another stood guard nearby—

Someone began to play the reed pipe again.

Bird that dwells in a mysterious tree

Rise to coast freely above the currents, along the edge of shadow and light, where the sun begins, cutting across the horizon, slicing through the upper ozone—rise above the pulse, along the invisible vein, and shine in your own galaxy, reveal the dust of life, cutting through the debris—now the emerald of the ocean winks at you from beneath—released from the strings that bind you, fall into the fathomless depths and sing as the knots of your self unwind.

Instructions for building a home—

These little bits of leaf and twig, acorn pieces and threads of bark are what you need to pick up one by one—carry them to a muffled spot on a high branch but close to the trunk—take a moment to think of a design but don't be too fussy (it should be aesthetically pleasing and uplifting while also homey and comfortable)—you might tilt it slightly towards the sunrise (which would help you with the ritual dawn song)—construct your nest in the tree of love, then warble forth for all to hear.

in bluegrey sunset the white bauhinia flowers sit up like beacons reflecting the halfmoonglow and the jacaranda blooms are suspended fluorescent stars in an unknowable algorithm—the patterns are murmurs across the nightening, woven from breath and an arc of rose-water, and framed by infinity across dimensions—one old man sits beneath this tree, having given up his worldly possessions, as the orchids seem to fall from the sky into his lap, and he smiles because he is the richest man in the world—a bumble-bee and floating petal vie for airspace barely avoiding collision, while crunching gravel increases in decibels and the weaving fluctuates—how did I get here, what is this stone that lays beneath my fingers and palms—in how many worlds can I weave a stone

Life (for K.A.)

She picked the verdant field, full of light—perhaps, out of the five options presented to her, this one reminded her of the gift, green and yellow with hints of blue, the earth on a seven centimetre card, a puzzle piece from the globe that he gave her on their wedding day. She picked the verdant field—a sign of the promises that belonged to them, the endless possibilities he saw in her, the dust from different continents that even now cling to the soles of her feet. The *antique,* the *numbers,* the *window,* the *waves,* the *field*—but she picked the verdant field—perhaps because he gave her hope, because she carries the world, because her heart is a rose—she chose life.

The tree line is not a line—that thins and thickens
depending on how fast life is speeding through this dream,
that takes heed of your inertia or your need
for perpetual motion—it is the view
from your window seat, the horizon
from the valley floor, a new world waiting
from the sea shore—

The tree line is verdure that wavers in the mist,
expands with the expansion of periwinkle skies,
is put to sleep by the gentle hands of delft,
and awakens with the dissipating night—
tree lines are a measure of sight and sound
hurtling past us—the unexpected accumulation
of quantum waves

Cypress

columns rippling with the air currents like marbled malachite, holding up the sky—they guard the heart of the mountain, their clawed feet digging into the earth, separating the landscape into spaces: one designated for thought and composition, another for prayer and meditation, yet another for painting the world with music—and each of these columns serves as a tower: if you look closely, little creatures make their way throughout their lifetimes, each branch protruding from a dark groove like a step ladder made to facilitate a better view—sometimes they travel along a branch, explore the level, the perspective, the street or residential area, and when the time comes they move on, ever climbing towards the sky

Ash

the cracked and dry mud is vertical—patched
with happy appearances of moss, harbouring
a trove of gem-like creatures—their bright red wing covers
a poor camouflage—in and out of these cracks
they scuttle, avoiding the keen eyes of birds
in the branches above, avoiding
the restlessness lurking around the roots
underneath—the cracked and dry mud
is vertical—connecting life to life
and earth to heaven

The Moon's Weaving (For M.D.)

She picked them up—those small small stones in the corner of the room—they called to her, their edges and smooth greyness resting against her palm—how many times had she contemplated the very ground from which they came, how many years had she longed to be in the room where they lay—this ache in her fingers seemed to grow sharper with each passing minute, as she tried to focus on the words and the joy of having attained this presence—the mild warmth of the sun through the window agitated aching limbs, glass shimmered, stones spoke—as she put them back the blanket of unease lifted and for that moment she sensed their joy—her love held her hand and led her out of the house passing beneath the window of that same room, both of them smiling and stepping lightly—*do not take me from my beloved* the moon sang softly as they walked away by the sea.

Rattling storms pierce the senses, pixelating dream fragments and sundering narrative seeds—you wander through a sea of red geranium as a wave of geranium and cypress rises high on one side, and the brilliance of colours floats around you and into a new dream—this is one you wish to stay in forever, so memory threads form and connections are welded while your heart tries to remain still, preparing for battle—storms begin to rattle again but this time you are ready—lift your hand from the soil that buries you, reach your fingers out, press your palm against the colour, a sign against the night.

Deodar

Needle-like leaves are strung and drooping as a patchy canvas
of blue-green suspended against a wall of other blues and greens—
a descendant of sacred places and ancient rituals, she finds herself
rooted in a different mountain where the lines are re-emerging,
where footsteps are a meditation and lend more power to the ley—

a woman draws near and pauses beneath the umbrella-like pines,
remembering every other time she has drawn near and halted—
for a moment the air is cool and clear, as though the sea is farther away,
at a higher altitude, and reminiscent of her ancestors' highlands—
she closes her eyes to better hear the hymn that is carried

across time—hands open and palms facing the world—
all she can hear is the rustling of cedar.

Afterword

'Come you lost Atoms to your Centre draw,
And be the Eternal Mirror that you saw,
Rays that have wander'd into Darkness wide
Return, and back into your Sun subside.'
Attar, 12th century (trans. Edward Fitzgerald)

There are times when I am moved to write in response to that feeling of wholeness, to consider the 'pale blue dot', as Carl Sagan dubbed it, and there are times when I find myself lost in the possibilities latent within its features and its inhabitants. And then there is that which connects everything, that which binds all these features, features like the forests and the oceans that precede us and survive us and in a way are witnesses to our comings and goings, to our interactions. In the nascent narratives of our world it is possible for their voices to inhabit our beings and our voices to inhabit their beings in a connection that gives us perspective, that allows us to shift our focus in and out of the picture so that, ultimately, no matter how far outside we go there is still something larger and no matter how deep within we travel there is still more to find—so that a tree can be a universe, an ocean a drop, and our planet an atom, or "a mote of dust suspended in a sunbeam" (Sagan, 1994).

Throughout my travels I have often been struck by the way that trees, in every landscape, signify a distinct narrative. But as I tried to write about them I found myself unable to isolate these signifiers from their context. I vacillated between metanarrative and micronarrative—the bigger picture and the smaller elements within the frame. In the end this collection came together as an exploration of the interplay between the segments and the whole, between the atoms and the sun, the light and the source—our attempt to discern the reality of things, the beauty of it all, the way we project and reflect how these segments can project onto and reflect each other.

Reference: Sagan, Carl. 1994. *Pale Blue Dot: A Vision of the Human Future in Space.* Random House. pg. 8

Acknowledgements

The following poems have been published previously:

Rain Dance and Layers—in Sangam House, India, 2017 http://poetry.sangamhouse.org/2017/05/niloofar-fanaiyan/
And then it rains—in 'Haifa', in *Cities: Ten Poets Ten Cities* (Recent Work Press, 2017)
Mirrors in the Garden— in Persian Passages, *Southerly Literary Journal*, Vol. 76, Num. 3, 2016

Niloofar Fanaiyan is a writer and poet who has lived in the U.S., Australia, the Netherlands, Tanzania and Israel. She was the 2016 Donald Horne Research Fellow at the Centre for Creative and Cultural Research, University of Canberra, where she obtained her PhD. She received the Canberra Critics Circle Literary Award for Poetry for her book of poems titled *Transit* (RWP, 2016).

2018 Editions
The Uncommon Feast **Eileen Chong**
Inlandia **KA Nelson**
Peripheral Vision **Martin Dolan**
The Love of the Sun **Matt Hetherington**
Moving Targets **Jen Webb**
Things I Have Thought to Tell You Since I Saw You Last **Penelope Layland**
The Many Uses of Mint **Ravi Shankar**
Abstractions **Various**

2017 Editions
A Song, the World to Come **Miranda Lello**
Cities: Ten Poets, Ten Cities **Various**
The Bulmer Murder **Paul Munden**
Dew and Broken Glass **Penny Drysdale**
Members Only **Melinda Smith** and **Caren Florance**
the future, un-imagine **Angela Gardner** and **Caren Florance**
Proof **Maggie Shapley**
Black Tulips **Moya Pacey**
Soap **Charlotte Guest**
Isolator **Monica Carroll**
Ikaros **Paul Hetherington**
Work & Play **Owen Bullock**

all titles available from
www.recentworkpress.com

www.ingramcontent.com/pod-product-compliance
Lightning Source LLC
Chambersburg PA
CBHW032050290426
44110CB00012B/1033